# HOW TO MOVE

*without losing
your mind ...
or the
remote control*

D0047681

# HOW TO MOVE

*without losing your mind ... or the remote control*

## BY KATHRYN TRAINOR

Acclaim Press™

**MORLEY, MISSOURI**

Acclaim Press
ACCLAIM PRESS, INC.
*Your Next Great Book*
P.O. Box 238
Morley, MO 63767
(573) 472-9800
www.acclaimpress.com

Book Design by:

Steward&Wise
GRAPHIC DESIGN

Designer: Ellen Sikes
Cover Design: Emily Sikes
Illustrator: Elizabeth Sikes
Photographer: Jo Reeves Photography

Library of Congress Cataloging-in-Publication Data

Trainor, Kathryn B., 1967-
How to move without losing your mind--or the remote control / by Kathryn Trainor.
p. cm.
ISBN-13: 978-1-935001-01-0 (alk. paper)
ISBN-10: 1-935001-01-9 (alk. paper)
1. Moving, Household. I. Title.
TX307.T73 2008
648'.9--dc22

2008016940

Printed in the United States of America
First printing: 2008
10 9 8 7 6 5 4 3 2 1

# CONTENTS

# DEDICATION

This book is dedicated to all the friends
who have packed, cleaned, babysat, cooked,
prayed, laughed, and cried with us
through each of our moves.

# ACKNOWLEDGEMENTS

Thank you to my Heavenly Father
for sending us on so many wild and
crazy adventures.

Thank you to my husband, Ted,
for believing in me and always dreaming
big dreams.

Thank you to our four "snuggle-bugs"
who fill our home with love and laughter
every day.

Thank you to my mom for being the
agent, sales team, and cheerleader for
this book.

*"He satisfies my desires with good things."*
*Psalm 103:5*

# HOW TO
# MOVE

*without losing
your mind ...
or the
remote control*

# Requirements for Membership in M.A.

This M.A. doesn't signify that Master of Arts degree I earned long ago, which is now lost in the bottom of a cardboard box marked "misc." This M.A. represents a support group called "Movers Anonymous." M.A. is for those of us who have packed one-too-many boxes and driven one-too-many miles, who have given away countless condiments and a plethora of popsicles, while cleaning out yet another refrigerator.

- ✓ Members of M.A. have license plates from two or more states as wall art.
- ✓ M.A. members know how it feels to pack a box, only

to have a toddler come along, dump the contents, and turn the box into a train or a fort.
- ✓ M.A. members have dry chapped hands from the cardboard, packing paper, and sticky tape.
- ✓ M.A. members have searched dumpsters, alleys, and liquor stores to find the perfect size cardboard boxes.
- ✓ M.A. members are always attending "going away" parties in which they are the honoree.
- ✓ M.A. members have lost at least one remote control in a move, but then found it in a box labeled "underwear drawer."

In the span of fifteen short years, our family has moved twelve times, lived in ten different cities and five states. Yes, that calculates to almost one move each year. I have attended one-too-many going away parties that were always for our family. I've driven thousands of miles, my eyes bleary with tears, grieving over what we have left behind. We have held too-many-to-count "moving sales" to downsize, and sometimes we even prepared for an upsize. Every town has been unique and every experience life-changing.

This is a book about survival - mental, emotional, and physical. May it bring you hope, humor, and practical helps in the midst of your own moving experience.

*-Kathryn Trainor*

## CHAPTER ONE

# To Keep or Not to Keep

**O**ne good thing about moving every year is that you have ample opportunity to de-clutter and organize your life, or at least make an attempt at it. Think before you pack! If you struggle with being a pack rat or you are overly sentimental about objects, ask a good friend to help you. Your friend can be objective and will aid you in thinking clearly.

Ask yourself the following questions:

- ✓ Will I really want to unpack this?
- ✓ Has it been more than a year since I have worn this outfit? Does it even fit?
- ✓ Have I ever really used this kitchen gadget?
- ✓ Do I have a use for it at my new home?

✓ If you are downsizing, ask yourself, "Will it fit in the next home?"

✓ Is there room for it in the moving truck?

✓ Why am I keeping this "what-not" that someone (I won't mention names, but we all have relatives who give odd gifts.) gave me in 1985 for Christmas? (Do you even know what it is or what to do with it?)

## The "Give Away" Box

My mom was great about always having a "give away" box in our home. It was continually being filled with outgrown clothes, unwanted toys, or other miscellaneous stuff. She instilled in us kids from an early age that there are people who don't have anything at all, who struggle just to make ends meet. She is a social worker at heart. She taught us that the coat we had outgrown could keep another child warm on a cold winter day. To this day that is probably why I love to give things away.

Every town has non-profit groups that need your un-needed or unwanted items. In turn, you will receive a receipt for your tax-deductible donation. Your books, tapes, and videos can be donated to the library. Your clothing and other household items can go to

Goodwill or a similar thrift store. Just look in the phone book under "social services" or "thrift shops" and you will see a multitude of agencies that need your help. Many of them will even come to your house to pick up your donation. Check out Appendix A at the end of this book for a list of nationwide agencies that need your unwanted items.

Maybe you also have special items you want to pass on to your children or grandchildren. Why keep packing them up and toting them from house to house, or state to state? If you designate recipients of those items in your will to be given to them after you die, then you miss out on the joy of seeing them receive it. If you give it to them now, then you can share the stories and traditions behind the heirloom.

## To Sell or Not to Sell

If you are moving to go to graduate school and will be living on little or no income or perhaps you are joining the Peace Corp, selling a few things is a good way to raise some much-needed cash. Perhaps you are downsizing for retirement purposes and your income is about to change drastically. Selling excess furniture, clothing, and decor will help you declutter and enhance your financial picture.

There are many different venues for selling, besides the traditional yard sale.

- ✓ Children's consignment stores are excellent for taking outgrown clothing, strollers, and toys. Some of them will even give you cash up-front for your items.
- ✓ Maybe you finally realize you will never be a size four ever again. Adult consignment stores will sell your designer clothing if it looks new and is still in style, or perhaps has become vintage or "retro."
- ✓ The local newspaper is an excellent resource for selling large items, such as a couch or a washing machine.
- ✓ Word of mouth is also a helpful tool. Let your friends and family know what you are selling and your desired price. They will tell everyone they know, or maybe a friend has secretly coveted the item all these years and will be the one to buy it from you.
- ✓ Antique dealers will also make cash offers for your

furniture or Grandma's china. Educate yourself; be sure you know the real market value of the item, and decide how little you will accept for payment. Keep in mind that you are the wholesaler.

✓ Stores that sell used cd's and dvd's will give you cash for your preowned music and movies.

✓ There are also specialized consignment stores selling anything from used furniture to sports equipment. Take a look in the phone book under "consignment."

✓ E-Bay has become very popular. If it seems too intimidating or time-consuming, there are storefronts that will sell your items for you on e-bay. They take a small percentage of the sale, but they are responsible for all of the work involved in selling (i.e. pictures and listing of the item, payment options, e-mail questions, shipping, etc).

✓ Pawn shops are not just for gamblers and drug dealers. Anyone, even a housewife and mom of four, can bring in household items to sell. I recently had my first pawn shop experience and learned the difference between a "pawn" and a "sell." Pawning is when you take out a loan on your item, then return to pick it up and pay for it with interest. A "sell" is a straightforward cash transaction for your used item.

## The Yard Sale

If you are going to have a yard sale, there are a few things you should know. Our cheap Saturday morning "entertainment" for years now has been attending yard sales. My four children can each find a new book or toy for 25 cents. Having moved so many times ourselves, we have "hosted" numerous garage sales.

Our first ever yard sale was when we combined our two "homes" to become one in marriage. My husband had this ugly set of brown earthenware pottery that I insisted he sell. He was a bit sentimental about it, but he agreed to sell it only if I sold my Blue Danube china that was given to me by my great aunt. Being foolish and in love, I agreed. Only years later did we

discover just how much my china was really worth. Needless to say, he gives me a piece of Blue Danube china for Christmas every year now.

The moral of that story is to make sure everyone involved agrees on what to sell. Here are a few hints and helps for the big sale:

- ✓ Signs are a must! Make it easy for people to find your house. Signs on main streets directing them to you, plus signs at every turn, are absolutely necessary. Make them large, colorful, and very easy to read.
- ✓ Ads in the newspaper are helpful, but not always necessary if you live near a busy road and have good signs.
- ✓ Do not price things individually. Save yourself some time by grouping similar items together. For example, put all the pants in one box and mark "50 cents per pair" on the box. We shoppers love to dig through piles to find buried "treasure."
- ✓ Now is NOT the time to be sentimental. Remember, these shoppers are hauling away your "stuff" for you. It may have been a $50 pair of pants at one time and you have great memories of dancing

the night away in those fancy red high heels, but now their combined value in the yard sale is about two dollars.

✓ Cleaning chemicals and yard pesticides cannot be packed in the moving truck. These are considered "hazardous materials" and will not be transported to your new abode. You can sell them cheaply or even give them away at your garage sale.

✓ Selling donuts, cokes, and coffee can boost your profits. We let our children set up their own version of a "lemonade stand" to sell snacks and drinks. This was especially successful the year our precocious three-year-old blue-eyed daughter was asking everyone, "Would you like to buy a Coke?" She might have a future in sales with her winsome personality.

✓ The early bird gets the worm. Some shoppers are on their way to work and have only a small window of time to hunt for bargains. They may also have a limited amount of money to spend, so open early and be the first place they stop to shop.

✓ Bargaining is good. Shoppers always like the feeling of "getting a good deal." Don't be offended when they offer you half of the sticker price. Ac-

cept their offer with a smile. Be thankful that you
don't have to haul that ugly green shag rug back
into your house at the end of the day.

✓ And when the day is over, whatever is left should
be donated to a local charity. Immediately place
unsold items in the trunk of your car, ready for
drop-off. Or call the charity that will come to your
home with their truck for pick-up. Don't even
think about bringing any of that old stuff back
into your clean, decluttered, and VERY organized
house!

## The Estate Sale

If you are downsizing from your 5,000 square foot
estate in the country to an apartment in Manhattan,
you have some serious decluttering to do. Or maybe
you have taken the vow of poverty and must sell all
of your belongings in order to move to a grass hut in
some faraway place. This would be the time to bring
in the "professionals." There are companies that will
organize an estate sale for you in your home. They do
all of the pricing, selling, and advertising for a fee.

## Children and Their Belongings

How is it that children have so many toys, clothes, and stuffed animals? We have been trying to get rid of one large stuffed orange dinosaur for years. He has been in three garage sales, but always manages to find his way back into the house before the end of the day. I suspect he has a secret accomplice.

Have you also noticed that stuffed animals reproduce in closets and toy boxes? They multiply as if they had traveled on Noah's Ark. Here are some clever ideas for ridding yourself of a few furry critters and the other multitude of playthings children acquire from Happy Meals and doting grandparents:

- ✓ My aunt came for a visit and offered to "buy" my children's unwanted toys, so that she could give them to a charity. They were willing to give up a few items in exchange for cold hard cash.
- ✓ On one move I suggested to my daughter that she use some of her stuffed animals as going away gifts for her friends. She chose a special one to give to each friend. She was ok with this since she knew they were going to a good home and would be cared for with love.

## How To Move

✓ It is important that children make their own decisions about what to sell or give away. Their attachment to a huge orange dinosaur is not for me to question. They know which toys, blankies, and other objects give them a feeling of comfort and security. On one move we misplaced my daughter's favorite nightlight. We had not thought about bringing it with us in the car, but instead it had been carefully wrapped and packed in some unmarked box. She could not sleep for many nights in our new home, because no other nightlight would do. Finally, that one particular box was unpacked and the beloved nightlight was found again.

## Just Throw it Out

Some items just belong in the trash can. You can't even give them away to the neediest of charities. Consider this an excellent opportunity to come clean.

We know a tragic story of some friends who had limited room in their moving truck. The husband was in charge of the truck loading. At the end of the day they had to leave some items behind that simply would not fit in the truck. One such piece was a cherished rocking chair. When they arrived at their new home (without the beloved rocking chair), they found that much room in the truck had been used to stock several huge boxes of plastic kitchen containers, the kind you wash out and reuse. The wife wished those boxes had been thrown out, so that her chair could have been on the truck.

Think long and hard before you pack. If you suffer from packrat-itis, get help! Here are some suggestions to get you started:

- ✓ Check the medicine cabinet. All expired medicines should be thrown out.
- ✓ How many plastic containers for leftovers can one family use? That collection of recycled plastic re-

ceptacles you have carefully washed, rinsed, and hoarded, but never used, has to go.

✓ Think long and hard before you pack up all of those old magazines. Are you really going to read them again?

✓ Examine the make-up in the bathroom drawer that you never wear. If it's old it could be harmful to your skin. Keeping it could be detrimental to your female beautification ritual.

✓ Why are you keeping receipts and bank statements from the 1960s? Save a tree by recycling all that paper, or buy an inexpensive shredder and use the output for packing materials.

# CHAPTER TWO

# Buy Low, Sell at the Right Price

There are entire books written on how to sell a house. They include lots of technical jargon and minute details about the process. My wisdom comes from someone who has "been there, done that" more often than the average homeowner. We have bought and sold all different sizes and varieties of homes, ranging in price from $75,000 to $675,000. We have become "experts" in what sells a house, and what definitely does not. Almost all of our homes have sold within the first thirty days, and some even in the first week.

Here are some important tips and ideas that have worked for us, time and time again:

✓ Price to sell. All of us overvalue our own home.

We all have sentimental memories and think our home is more wonderful than all the others, when in fact we have not seen all the other homes, and we have no idea what kind of competition we are up against. Honestly, we all want to make a profit, but sometimes we need to be thankful we were able to break even or to just get rid of the property. Owning two homes is not fun. When I was eight months pregnant with our third child, we were in that predicament. Paying two mortgages and two sets of utility bills is bad enough, but you should have seen me out there mowing two lawns in the summer heat. It's impossible to be objective when it comes to pricing. Find a wise realtor who will give you a realistic picture of the real estate market and tell you what your home is actually worth. If it seems a little low to you (and to your emotions), then it is probably priced right.

✓ Retain a realtor. We all think we can save a little money by selling our home ourselves. We have done this just one time in all of our twelve moves around the country, and it was a lot of work and emotional stress. In reality, I am not sure how much money we saved by the time we printed flyers, bought signs, and advertised in the newspaper and on the internet. An excellent realtor will be worth every penny. Real estate agencies spend lots of money on advertising plans, and they know what is happening in the real estate market. A good realtor is also an amazing negotiator. We have saved more money and made more money on both buying and selling, because we had realtors who knew how to negotiate. On the rare occasion you may have undervalued your home, a studious realtor has access to statistics and can advise you on the fair market value. A good real estate agent also spends time meeting with the home inspector and then arranging for the roofer or plumber or carpet cleaner, or whatever other service is required, for the sale to be completed. Ask around for a realtor with an excellent reputation and success rate.

✓ Curb appeal matters. On our last house hunt we looked at over eighty homes in our price range. Sometimes we took one look and kept right on driving. Think of the buyer as someone who will ALWAYS "judge a book by its cover." If the grass is knee-deep and the shutters are coming loose, the potential buyer estimates that the inside must look even worse. Not only should you mow the grass and weed the flower beds, but you need to plant some, fresh colorful flowers. Remove those cobwebs from the front porch; add a new welcome mat and a beautiful wreath on the door. If your shutters are faded, then paint them. Everything on the outside of your home should be "calling" the buyer to step inside. You don't want to be a "drive-by" house.

✓ Smells will make or break you. Ask someone who can be objective, and brutally honest, to walk through your house and sniff for odd odors. Closets with shoes can be especially putrid. A bad smell will make a buyer turn and run. Invest a few dollars in some cans of room deodorizers that "neutralize" the air. But do not over-do it with flowery smells that overpower the senses, cause headaches, and induce asthmatic or allergic reactions. Keep in mind that pregnant women are known for their extraordinary olfactory sense. Some smells are universally pleasing, like fresh baked bread or chocolate chip cookies. Make your home memorable for its good smells, not bad ones.

Having the carpets cleaned is an excellent means of adding good smells and removing old stale ones. One "memorable" house we looked at had a fancy billiard room. When we opened the door to check it out, the smell of smoke was so thick it caused a full-blown asthma attack in my husband. Needless to say, that house was on the market for a very long time.

✓ Check the walls. Remember that time someone bumped into the wall with a golf club or the swinging baseball bat? Or those smeared fingerprints where children walk down the hallway? Do a thorough check of all walls and, hopefully, you have a can of paint to cover old smudges and to make your home look new again. Sometimes an entire room will need a fresh coat of bright neutral paint, especially if your foyer has been painted country mauve since the 1980's. Another handy helper is the "magic eraser." You will be amazed at how it can clean little Molly's "artwork" off the bedroom wall and remove the fingerprints made by sticky hands.

✓ A little packing goes a long way. Get a jumpstart on your packing by boxing up all of your personal items and family portraits. In order for the potential buyer to "picture" themselves living there, your home must be emptied of anything that says it belongs to you. Pack up all the clutter and bric-a-brac. Clear off all flat surfaces (i.e. countertops, dressers, tables). Your home should look and feel like a decorator showcase home. Remember, less is more. We know friends who rented a storage space to put their extra furniture and boxes, just so their home would appear bigger and less cluttered. If your home seems bare to you, that translates into "spacious" for the potential buyer.

✓ Store your clutter. There are many different options for storage nowadays. There is probably a "store-it-yourself" business near you. Even the most remote small towns have one nowadays. On one of our moves our realtor had a moving truck we could use for free; that truck saved us lots of money. We were able to clear out many extra boxes and furniture to turn our home into a showcase home. You can move some furniture to your new location or store items at a friend's home or in a grandparent's garage. There are also PODS (large storage containers) that can be parked in your driveway, or even moved to another location.

Look in your local phone book under "storage" and you will be overwhelmed by the options.

✓ Then pack some more. Do you know that saying, "One man's junk is another man's treasure"? Well, in the case of selling a house, your "treasure" may look like junk to someone else. We once looked at a home that had a bedroom full of collectible "treasures." There were at least 5,000 dolls on the bed, shelves, dresser, floor, and all around the room. I have to tell you it gave us a very creepy feeling, all those eyes staring at us. We couldn't get out of that house fast enough.

✓ Add instant ambience. Good lighting is essential. Make sure all light fixtures, both indoor and outdoor, have new bulbs with the highest wattage possible. We don't normally live with one-hundred-dred-watt bulbs in all of our lamps, but when we get ready to sell a house, we do. When you know you are about to have a "showing," turn on all the lights and add some soft classical music in the background. Be sure blinds are open to display the wonderful views and to let in the sunshine.

✓ Clean up before each showing. I certainly understand how hard it is to keep a house clean 24/7 with four children and a husband. I have learned some simple ways to hide the laundry and clear the countertops at the last minute. Keep a rag and some cleaner under the kitchen sink for a quick swipe of all surfaces. You also can conveniently store cleaning supplies under every bathroom sink, depending on how large your home is. This quick clean will also leave a fresh scent. Keep some air neutralizer spray in the closet and give every closet a "treatment" before heading out the door. Hide extra "stuff" under the couch or in the dryer. Don't hide things in the washing machine, because we have been known to forget about it and then turned it on when it was filled with something other than clothes! Get the husband and children in on the action. Everyone can be responsible for making up their own bed, hiding clutter under their bed, and turning on the lights in their rooms. I know one clever realtor who made a "contract" for the children to sign. The contract said that if they helped sell the house by keeping their "area" clean, then they would make a designated amount of money (like $50) when the house sold.

✓ Go the extra mile. With each of our homes I have made a "scrapbook" for the potential buyer. No, it's not a book about you and your adorable children enjoying the backyard, nor is it about how many of your cute kids were born in this house. It should contain practical and helpful information. Use a simple three ring binder, or scrapbook, and fill it with clear pocket pages. Fill the pages with useful information, such as neighborhood covenants and restrictions. You also may want to type up a list of the nearest parks, grocery stores, pharmacies, and other resources. This helps the buyer visualize the excellent location of your home. If you spent money on those fancy real wood plantation shutters (like we have), then you want the buyer to see just how much they cost. Include receipts for big home projects, like the new granite countertops or the fancy wrought-iron fence. When you sell the home, the new owners will appreciate knowing who did the work and whom to call for their warranty. Also, don't think this will get you more money for your home, but it will give you an edge over the competition.

## Fluffy and Fido

You may be one of those animal lovers who adore your pets and treat them like royalty. Not everyone is like you. Now would be a good time to send Fluffy and Fido on their dream vacation. Ask a good friend to keep them temporarily while you are trying to sell your home. Buyers with allergies will run the other way if they see a cat or a dog. We know because we have both asthma and allergies. We have been turned off from buying many a home because the pet smells were so strong. At the very least, keep your pets outside and well-contained.

Many families bring children along on their house-hunting adventures. Some young children will scream in terror if they hear a dog bark. It is difficult to think about buying a house when your children are clinging to you and crying uncontrollably.

On one of our home shopping adventures the owners had gated their dog inside one of the bedrooms. Not only were we unable to climb the gate to finish our house tour, but the poor dog had relieved himself on the floor of the room. Needless to say, we did not purchase that house.

## Important Housing Details

Be sure you call every utility company (phone, water, electric, gas, etc.) to tell them what day to discontinue your service. No matter how desperately you want to save a few pennies, do NOT turn it off too soon. On moving day you WILL need the water to be running, the air conditioner to work, and the electricity on for the vacuum cleaner. If you move out before the new owner takes possession of your home, all utilities must be on for the home inspections and remain on until the day of the real estate closing. As a back-up plan, I like to make a list of all the utility companies and their phone numbers in case I need to change the service dates. Giving utility companies your forwarding address allows them to return your deposit to you. You will find blank worksheets in Appendix B and Appendix C to help you with this.

Turning on the utilities at your new location for the day you move is also extremely important. Once again, working bathrooms and air conditioning are vital to everyone's comfort. The fish tank needs electricity, too, if the fish survived the car ride.

Remember to notify the post office of your change of address. They even have their own special website to assist you.

www.moversguide.usps.com

Here's a quick checklist (See Appendix B and Appendix C for worksheets.):

✓ Turn on utilities at new home BEFORE you arrive.
✓ Turn off utilities at old house, but not too soon.
✓ Notify the post office.

✓ Provide your new address to your old job for that
final paycheck, or for tax purposes.

Change the address on all magazine subscrip-
tions, credit cards, life insurance, and BILLS (Even
though you are tempted to not do this last one, it
would be bad for your credit rating to not provide
your forwarding address).

# CHAPTER THREE

# Box It or Leave It

After you rid yourself of some clutter, you can begin to pack. Every moving experience needs a good packing plan. Packing should never be a one-woman task, no matter how much of a "control freak" you are. Believe me, it takes one to know one. Now is not the time to be "superwoman." Moving is an emotionally exhausting experience for the whole family, so it's important to have physical assistance. After twelve moves I have actually learned a thing or two, though I am still pretty hard-headed and stubborn most of the time. Almost all of our moves have been on a tight budget, without any professional assistance.

## Boxes, boxes, boxes

These Cardboard boxes are really quite costly.

Retail stores now have "cardboard only" recycling dumpsters. The boxes are clean and already broken down, thus fitting easily into the trunk of your car. Some might call this "dumpster diving"; however, you are helping with the recycling process by utilizing this great resource. Liquor stores also have excellent size boxes for books, and the boxes are quite sturdy. On your box-hunting adventure bring a knife to break down boxes. More will fit in your vehicle if they are flattened first. You should see me trying to fit empty cardboard boxes in my minivan between four children and their car seats.

Don't be afraid to ask neighbors and friends, or your realtor, if they know of anyone who has recently moved and is unpacking. You can assist them by taking the used boxes and packing paper off their hands; this saves them a trip to the dump and provides them a feeling of resourcefulness. You might also get a chance to swap moving stories and empathize with one another.

If you don't like the idea of "used" boxes, or you need a lot of boxes in a hurry, then you can purchase boxes locally at self-storage facilities or rental truck companies. You still have the problem of fitting them into your vehicle. Those wardrobe boxes are bigger than you imagine. I have recently learned of a website that will deliver boxes to your door. The address is www.moveout.com and they promise to have the lowest prices and free shipping. I need to try this on our next move.

If you know you're going to be moving a lot, then you might want to invest in several large plastic storage tubs. The ones with the red lids help me keep track of all of our Christmas decorations. The box with the orange lid was for Thanksgiving stuff, but I can't seem to find it this year. If you send your husband to the attic for a particular box, the clear kind where you can see the contents are quite helpful. "Under the bed" storage boxes make superb use of small spaces, which is an especially good idea if you have to "downsize."

## Labeling

Though it may appear that I am stating the obvious, the act of labeling is actually quite complicated. Packing is like putting pieces together in a puzzle, but not always the parts of the same puzzle. Maybe you meant to put all the coffee mugs in one box combined with the coffee maker, but then you found one mug left in the dishwasher. It happens to be your husband's favorite, so very carefully you pack it in an open space in the corner of the box of Grandma's china. This may not seem like a big deal, until you decide Grandma's china isn't worth unpacking at the next house. The favorite coffee mug is now M.I.A. in the stacks of attic boxes.

- ✓ Use permanent marker. It won't fade in the attic heat or wash off in the rain (yes, it has been known to rain on moving day).
- ✓ Be specific! You think you will remember what is in each box, but after the emotional upheaval of your life, you'll be trying hard just to recall your own name and how many children you have, not to mention where they are at the moment.
- ✓ The remote control seems to be the most commonly lost item, so write it in BIG letters on the outside of the box. You might want to skip packing it altogether and just stick it in the glove compartment of your car. But make yourself a note about where you put it, because you will most assuredly forget that you put it in such a "handy" place.

## How To Move

- ✓ Never, EVER, mark a box "misc." Enough said.
- ✓ Small fragile items (like the dainty lid to the antique teapot that has been passed down in your family for three generations), wrapped in paper, can take on the appearance of a wad of trash. Be sure to write on the paper, "Don't throw away!" Also, write detailed notes to yourself on the outside of the box.
- ✓ Be wary of using sticker labels that might peel off in the heat, or wash off in the rain. Speaking from experience, tiny fingers like to scratch, pick, and peel stickers off boxes. The good old-fashioned permanent marker is really the way to go.
- ✓ Permanent markers do run out of ink, or fall inside a box being packed, so buy plenty. (And if you're trying to sell your house, don't allow your children to write with permanent markers on the driveway. Speaking from experience, it does NOT wash off.)

## Helping Hands

Everyone needs to get in on the action when it comes to packing. Assigning certain areas to family members is very important. Sharing the load is the key to everyone's happiness, especially Momma's.

✓ Children, at any age, can actually pack their own rooms. Give them a box and let them fill it; however, they do need some instructions. For example, be sure they know that their clothes can stay in their dresser, since the movers will move them that way. Before taping a child's packed box closed, be sure to check it and then label it. Children will enjoy the responsibility and the ownership of packing their belongings; additionally, it keeps children busy and out of the way. Packing also helps "little ones" understand the moving process. (Important note: If there's a toy you've been hoping to "lose" and losing it won't cause serious psychological trauma to your child, now is the time for it to mysteriously "get lost.")

✓ Husbands can pack the garage and yard. They can also be responsible for their own closet. Give them something to do and they will rise to the occasion. Books are also a pretty safe packing item for the men. Books don't have to be wrapped in paper and they don't break when dropped.

✓ Girlfriends are excellent packers. One dear friend in Atlanta actually has "the gift of packing," and boy is she amazing! You should have seen her pack my four sets of china in record time. Getting a group together to pack can be a party. Crank up the music, bring out the lemonade and cookies, and in no time at all the packing is finished. Women love any excuse for a "girls night out," especially for the sake of "ministry" and to serve a sister in need. During one especially difficult move from our "dream home," my friends secretly wrote notes on the inside flaps of the boxes as they packed. When I arrived at my new home and began to unpack, I was surprised and delighted to find my boxes covered with funny jokes, drawings, and words of encouragement.

✓ Professional packers can be costly, but so can breaking that Waterford crystal vase. Movers will often only insure the items that they have packed for you. A quality packer will use LOTS of paper and has been trained to perform amazing feats of packing in a short amount of time. You may also choose a partial pack, where the professionals are hired to take care of all fragile or unusual items.

## More Packing Tips

People always ask me, how do you get it all done so fast? The good thing about moving a lot is that you can get better at it. I have learned some tricks and ideas over the years that have simplified our experience.

✓ Wardrobe boxes are a must. Don't take clothes off the hangers, but instead simply hang them in this specially equipped box. This will save you lots of time.
✓ Never remove hangers. Since wardrobe boxes are expensive, I save money by also using regular boxes. I can pack our hall closet by carefully

laying the coats, with hangers still intact, in a regular box. When I am ready to unpack, I lift them out by their hangers and hang them back up immediately. The same can be done with children's clothes.

✓ Pick a central packing area. Having one main location for tape, paper, and markers simplifies the process and keeps the mess to a minimum. You won't waste time trying to remember which room you left the tape in, or wonder where your permanent marker went. And you will have only one spot in the house that is a "mess" with packing supplies. Be sure to choose a space that is not in a heavy traffic area; our dining room table is usually the perfect spot for us.

✓ Pack similar items together. Try not to mix things up from one room to the next. If it is your son's stuff and you know it will all go into his room at the next home, then keep it all together.

✓ Think of the future. Keep in mind what rooms you will have in your new home. Maybe next time you will have a study or an exercise room. Will the children share a room or have their own this time? The fancy lamps you are planning to use in the new living room should be packed together. Always think about how you will be unpacking it at the next house.

# CHAPTER FOUR

# Truckin' on Down the Road

## Choosing the Mode of Transport

**N**ow is the time to decide whether you will move everything in your brother-in-law's pick up truck or hire a professional moving company. We have experienced everything from do-it-yourself rental trucks to caravans of our friends' vehicles. Over the years we have learned to save our pennies and use whatever money we can scrape together to hire a professional moving company.

There are many different options for transporting your precious possessions from point A to point B. I will tell you a few of our fiascos and let you make your own decision.

## Freebies

Everyone has a friend who has a friend who has a truck or large van. This will certainly be the most frugal means of moving, but it will also cost you a lot of time. The longest moves seem to be across town rather than across the United States. All those millions of trips carrying just a few boxes here and there can be wearisome. The time we moved from an apartment to our first home took months. You can't fit that many boxes in a two-door sports car, so there were many drives back and forth.

The problem with larger vehicles, which are generally open bed trucks, is the unforeseen inclement weather. It always seems to rain on moving day. However, if you don't have any money, then this could be your only option. Borrow a very large tarp from your friends who like to camp, and then obtain lots of bungee cords.

## The Rental Truck

When sizing up which truck to rent, be sure you know just how much stuff you can fit in it. Also, plan to round up enough friends to help you load and unload.

Be sure you understand every nuance of the equipment you are using; don't assume you know how to drive a truck or hook up a trailer. On one of our first cross- country moves we chose to rent a truck and haul our car on a rented trailer connected to the rear of the truck. Apparently we had not hooked up the trailer correctly and the brakes just happened to be on the entire time we were driving.

Several hours and many miles down the road, we glanced in the rearview mirror and noticed a small fire leaping up from behind us. We quickly pulled over to discover that the trailer wheel had caught fire after being dragged with the brake locked for so many miles. As any athletic man would, my husband first attempted to put out the fire by throwing the ice cubes from our cooler. When that didn't work, we extinguished the flames by frantically squirting them with the juice boxes we had packed. I recommend packing a fire extinguisher instead.

## The Professionals

I will scrape together whatever money I can, even go without food for a week, in order to hire a professional moving company. The doctor bills for the "thrown-out-back" and the years of therapy for the stress caused by moving ourselves cost us more than hiring professionals. For our family, it is worth the expense.

There is a plethora of movers, so obtain quotes from several moving companies; and don't just settle for the one with the best price. Remember the saying, "You get what you pay for." One mover gave us a bargain price, so we chose his company. We did not realize it was a bargain only because his truck was smaller than the rival company's truck. He had underestimated how our belongings would fit on his truck. On moving day we were stuck with either giving away furniture (which we did) or finding a means of moving it ourselves. It was quite a traumatic experience.

Movers have distinct reputations, both good and bad. Ask your friends whom they would recommend. People enjoy talking about their moving experiences; it's therapeutic for them and informative for you. Your experienced realtor will also have some well-informed ideas and advice for you.

The internet is also full of resources about movers. Learn as much you can before trusting someone with Great Grandma's heirloom rocker or china hutch. Here are just a few of the available websites to keep yourself informed:

www.moving.com
www.getamover.com
www.movingscam.com

Movingscam.com provides a current "blacklist" of moving scams that have happened across the country. Be sure to check that out. Movingscam.com also gives the following helpful advice:

✓ Find a local moving company that has been in business at least ten years.

✓ Pick three companies and have them come to your house to provide an in-home estimate.

✓ Do NOT simply hire a company off the internet. Movingscam.com reports that most victims of fraud found their mover on the internet.

✓ Ask if they do the moving themselves or if they sub-contract.

✓ Check out their trucks and storage facility, and maybe even visit their office. Are their trucks permanently marked with the company's name?

Do not hire a moving broker, because current consumer protection laws apply only to "Motor Carriers" and not to "Household Goods Brokers."

# CHAPTER FIVE

# The Day of the Big Move

## Last Minute Packing

"Just say no" to last minute packing! That "one more thing" really will not fit in your car or in the moving truck. You can't even imagine the things we've had to leave behind, because they simply would not fit. We've given away more furniture than I care to recall, and we almost had to leave children (not really, but the fish barely made it).

## Packing the Car (or mini-van or suv)

You can pack the car the night before the big day. Be sure to plan for suitcases with a change of clothes and important toiletries and every emergency medicine you think you might possibly need.

✓ Don't forget pillows, favorite stuffed animals, and sleeping bags. Moving trucks never arrive at your destination when they say they will, so be prepared for a day or two of "camping" in an empty abode.

✓ More than just a change of clothes is needed, because even the best of moving companies can be days late.

✓ Nightlights are critical for children. A lamp or two is also a good idea.

✓ If you are grumpy without your morning coffee, then you better pack the coffee maker, too. Remember to include all the supplies that go with it (filters, coffee, sugar, cream, and a mug to drink it from.)

✓ If you want to take a shower or bath at your new home (and you remembered to have the water turned on), pack plenty of towels and probably a shower curtain.

✓ Speaking of the bathroom, don't forget the toilet paper.

✓ It's also a good idea to include a few games or activities for the children, especially since you may not have any friends at your new destination to babysit your children for you.

✓ Cleaning supplies need to go with you in the car. You will be using them right away at your new home.

✓ The toolbox also must be packed in the car. If you want your tables and beds put back together again at your destination, tools are essential to the process.

✓ Important papers MUST be in the car with you. Invest in a plastic file box and put all of your most important papers in it. This can be everything from birth certificates to marriage license to insurance policies.

✓ Now the car is becoming rather full, but make sure you leave a space for a box of tissues. At the end of this exhausting day, and after some emotional goodbyes, you will be shedding a few tears. At the very least you'll be sneezing, or have a runny nose and watery eyes, from all the dust that has been kicked up.

*(See Appendix D for a handy checklist to use when packing all of the items listed above.)*

## The Dilemma of Children

Children need something to do, or somewhere to go, on the "big day," and preferably someplace safe. On one of our more memorable moving days, we thought it would be a good idea for the children to stay out of the way by playing on the neighbor's trampoline. As my husband was lifting one of the children onto the trampoline he threw out his back and was immobile and horizontal the rest of the day. You can just imagine how much help he was on that move.

Get creative and enlist the assistance of your friends. One particularly hot summer a dear friend drove my children around town for eight hours, watching movies and eating meals in our air conditioned mini van equipped with a DVD player.

Here are a few more ideas to keep your sanity (and your children alive):

- ✓ Ask a friend to keep them at his or her house for the day.
- ✓ Several friends could take shifts - someone invites them over for breakfast, then another picks them up for lunch, and then another friend has them for dinner.

- ✓ If they are school-age and it's not summertime, let a friend pick them up after school and take them to their house.
- ✓ Take them to the movies, or to a park, or any other activity that might be time-consuming and far away from the chaos of moving day.
- ✓ Send them out-of-town for an overnight with grandparents or friends.
- ✓ DON'T ask someone to watch them at YOUR house.

Here's the perfect example of why NOT to do this: When our youngest was two years old, we were living in Atlanta. The front door of our home was propped open for furniture and boxes coming and going. It had been awhile since we had done a "head count" on the children, and it was way past lunchtime. That's another thing, children are ignored and not likely to be fed on moving day. Someone said they were hungry, so we began to gather the children for a feeding frenzy. No one could find the two-year-old anywhere. That's when we thought of the front door. We were terrified that he had perhaps wandered outside and could be anywhere in the big city. My husband was the first to reach the front door and saw something in the distance. A closer look revealed that our son had climbed into the moving truck with his plastic push mower and was "mowing" the inside of the truck.

## Nourishment

You will need to eat at some point, but you won't have any food in the pantry, and the refrigerator will be unplugged and loaded on a truck. Here is yet another opportunity for friends to help out.

You can't leave the movers, because they need lots of instructions about what to load on the truck and what NOT to stack on top of the antique mahogany dresser. You will also be amazed at what they are able to unscrew and take apart, only later to be told by you that it was an item that actually needed to stay with the house. You also need to stay close by when they are taking beds apart, so that you can gather up all the nuts, bolts, and screws. Just this year we finally broke down and bought new screws for the missing "few" in our boys' bunk beds. Thankfully, the beds never fell on them.

Be sure your cell phone is charged and handy, because the phones are probably packed, and service may be turned off already. Call those faithful friends and ask them to bring snacks or sandwiches and drinks. You're probably ready for a glass of wine by now, but now is not the time.

## Cleaning

The "universal movers handbook" (this doesn't really exist) states that it is common courtesy to clean the home for the next inhabitant. And if you're a renter, cleaning is a must if you want your deposit back. Following behind the movers, you can clean each room as they clear it out. This is also a good way to make sure that nothing is forgotten, like some out-of-the-way attic space behind a secret door that had fifty more boxes that they did not see. Yes, this too has happened to us. After a room is clean, you can shut the door to signify that it is finished.

This is a terrific opportunity for the friend who does not have "the gift of babysitting," but is perhaps good with a broom or mop. We had one very type-A childless friend who made perfectly straight and even rows in all of our carpets as he vacuumed. Our carpets never looked so good. I hope the next homeowners noticed.

# CHAPTER SIX

# Special Delivery

**Y**ou have made it to your destination and you are waiting for the moving van to arrive. At this point you may be doing some cleaning, depending on how "courteous" the previous residents were. Be prepared to tell the movers exactly where to put every box and each piece of furniture.

- ✓ Have a measuring tape handy, so you can figure where your furniture is going to fit (or not). If you want a piece of furniture centered along a wall, then the measuring tape is good for that, too.
- ✓ Make big signs and tape them to the bedroom doors, so the movers will know what goes where.
- ✓ Keep those cleaning supplies handy. You'll be seeing your furniture from new angles. You may

even be amazed at the cobwebs, dust, and "science experiments" growing on the underside of things, no matter how much of a perfect housekeeper you have been. Some corners have simply been un-reachable until moving day.

✓ Tools are very important. Anything you needed (like screwdrivers, specialized wrenches, or drills, to take things apart) will be necessary to put everything back together again. Surprisingly, the movers do not always have these tools, so it's up to you to have them handy.

✓ If you want your icemaker or washing machine to work, this will also require special tools and someone who knows how to do it.

✓ Remember the nuts, bolts, and screws, for the crib, beds, and tables? I hope you haven't lost them already, because you need to have them ready. Hopefully you put them in a plastic bag or container and made sure to label them, because you need to know which fasteners attach to which piece of furniture.

## Furniture Placement

All day long everyone will be asking you, "Where

do you want this?" You have to be able to think quickly. When you can't think, you will probably say, "Oh, just put that in the garage." If you are not careful, by the end of the day EVERYTHING will be stacked in the garage.

Plan ahead for the placement of your furniture. Take measurements and have some general ideas about where items will fit. My mother likes to study the new house plan and use an architect's ruler to place her furniture prior to moving day. I am not quite that organized or exact, but I do have a good idea of where everything is going to fit.

Get creative in your furniture placement. Try to think outside the box.

✓ Utilize your closets. When space is small, we put shelves and dressers inside our bedroom closets. More than once, we have even been known to turn a closet into an office or sewing room, fully equipped with a desk and a lamp. We have removed closet doors to make a room appear bigger, or to add a creative play area for children. One time I created a "kitchen" in my daughter's closet, complete with wallpaper and all her plastic appliances. I hung a mirror over her "sink", added curtains, and it took on the appearance of a real kitchen window.

✓ Create kitchen storage. When the kitchens have been too small, and had only minimal cabinet space, we have brought in other furniture to add storage. A bookshelf in the kitchen can look very decorative, holding plates and glasses. We have also used a dresser in the kitchen for storing table linens and paper products.

✓ Be creative. Every home is unique. Maybe this time your dining room is small or non-existent. A china cabinet placed in your bedroom can make an attractive dresser. Colorful sweaters displayed behind the glass doors add color and texture to the room. The drawers and cabinet below are handy, just like a traditional dresser.

## Children

Here again, there is the challenge of children. To stay out of the way of moving furniture and far from open doors and busy streets, children need to be corralled and kept occupied. Now is a good time to bring out the TV and some movies. For your sanity and their safety, it is wise to set aside a particular area for them to play. Be specific and rigid in your boundaries for their time of quarantine. This is good in theory, but it won't always happen like you planned.

Case in point, on delivery day we happened to misplace our youngest child, once again. It was mid-afternoon, and I decided to check on the children in their "play area" where they seemed very quiet and content; however, upon counting heads I discovered there were only three, instead of the usual four. We began an all-out search for the two-year-old, calling his name upstairs and downstairs, but no answer. Just as we were beginning to panic, we heard a noise from the downstairs den. Providentially, he snores when he is in a deep sleep. Following the sound of sawing zzz's, we found him curled up asleep in a hidden corner of the couch.

For obvious reasons, it is infinitely better if a friend offers to babysit your children. Another safe option is they could still be enjoying that vacation with the protective, indulgent grandparents.

## Window Treatments

Here is one of those crazy things that may not have occurred to you. Sometimes the previous owner of a home will take the expensive designer custom draperies, curtains, or blinds with them to their next house. If you are moving to a newly constructed home, there are definitely no blinds on the windows. Unless you enjoy flashing your neighbors or like to wake up with the sun, you need to have a plan. This has caught us by surprise more than once. Hardware stores sell paper shades that have adhesive to adhere to the window frame. My husband has had lots of practice hanging mini blinds. On our last move, we got smart and had him go to the house first to hang blinds, before we ever moved in.

Once when we moved to Tennessee to a newly built home, our very generous and thoughtful neighbors across the street brought us a pile of old sheets, nails, and a hammer to use for temporary curtains. I guess they didn't want to see us in our pajamas.

## CHAPTER SEVEN

# Home Sweet Home

The moving truck is gone and you are surrounded by boxes. Everyone is tired and emotionally drained, but you can't live in cardboard forever. You have to find sheets for the beds and clothes for work. You can't eat on paper plates forever, so the kitchen must be unpacked soon.

## Unpacking

Unpacking follows the same rules as packing; everyone has a part to play. You will drive yourself crazy, and everyone around will despise you, if you try to do it all yourself. Unpacking day is NOT the time to be bossy. Emotions are running high and the exhaustion factor is still huge, since no one ever sleeps well in new surroundings.

- ✓ Children are excellent at unpacking their own rooms. Not only does this keep them busy, but they can take ownership of their new space. This is an excellent means of teaching responsibility, as well as organization. My children always tell me that unpacking their rooms is like Christmas to them. Opening boxes is just like unwrapping presents.

- ✓ Husbands enjoy staying out of the way, so let them organize the garage and outdoor areas. They are also capable of unpacking their own underwear and shoes, and don't let them tell you otherwise. Also, someone needs to break down all those boxes and take them to the dump. Men are all over that.

- ✓ Girlfriends are excellent at unpacking and helping to decide where to put things. Having an objective set of eyes can help you see new possibilities for organization. I taught my best friend to put her underwear in one of the bathroom drawers. She thought it was ingenious and has thanked me for it ever since.

- ✓ Professional movers also offer unpacking services. My friend had her whole kitchen unpacked in a few hours by the pros. This sounds like a dream come true to me. If you are particular about where to place items or just on a really tight budget, you may choose to do it yourself.

## Eating

Our families do need nourishment and sometimes it's not easy to come by. You might have a sweet neighbor who greets you with a plate of warm chocolate chip cookies, but those kinds of neighbors seem few and far between in today's world. If you move to Orlando, Florida, I have a dear friend who still does this for her neighbors. (She would probably even offer to unpack a box or watch your kids for you.)

Personally, I don't think much about food when I'm faced with the stress of moving. I can become quite preoccupied and overly obsessed with the placement of boxes and creatively fitting furniture into small spaces; however, husbands and children become grumpy and whiney when they are not fed. This can be a real hindrance in the whole moving experience.

When we moved to Memphis with a toddler and a six-month-old baby, my husband  left at 5am the next morning for a business trip. I was alone in an empty house with two small children for what seemed like months, but actually was only five days. The movers arrived days later than we had originally planned and the refrigerator we had ordered was a week later than expected. Thankfully, McDonalds serves breakfast (and lunch and dinner).

- ✓ Convenience foods are essential. Snack foods can keep you going for days. Now is not the time to monitor calories or worry about how many servings of fruits and vegetables everyone is eating. This is survival mode; however, do beware of those fatal sugar highs and lows. And drink plenty of water; dehydration will most certainly inhibit the success of moving day.
- ✓ Paper products are your friend. You don't want dirty dishes piling up in a kitchen already overflowing with stacks of boxes. Use paper plates, plastic utensils, and throw-away cups.
- ✓ Make sure you know where all the closest fast food restaurants are. Hopefully, your new hometown has some sort of semblance of a restaurant, even if it's just the deli bar at the local supermarket.

✓ Pizza delivery is an excellent source of nutrition, and you don't have to waste time driving to get it. Believe it or not, where we live now actually does not have pizza delivery service, so appreciate it while you have it.

✓ If there's no refrigerator yet, a cooler of ice is pretty handy. If it's a cold winter, you can keep refrigerated items on the back porch, but be mindful of outdoor critters. On one hot southern summer move, our thoughtful new neighbors brought us a cooler filled with ice, cold water, and sodas.

✓ Meals from your new neighbors and friends are the greatest gift when you haven't unpacked any kitchen boxes. During one of our moves meals were brought to us for the entire first week of our transition experience. It was freeing to not have to think about grocery shopping or finding the box with the can opener in it.

## Children

Keeping children busy in the midst of the chaos is no small task. It will require at least a minimal amount of your attention. The boxes you have unpacked make excellent entertainment. One time my children all became dogs and each had his or her own "doghouse" box. They decorated their doghouses and we cut all kinds of doors and windows in them. The barking became annoying after awhile, but at least there was no whining or arguing. Use your imagination; our boxes have become trains, houses, and entire towns.

Another superb source of fun is the packing materials. Those packing bubbles can be "popped" for hours. The noise of four children, or eight little feet, stomping on air bubbles is a bit loud, so you can make them go outside for this activity. It works better on the driveway anyway. The packing paper is excellent for all kinds of craft projects and drawings. Another fun game is to have a "snowball" fight with wadded up paper. They are white like snow, but won't melt and make a mess on your new hardwood floors. Whoever has the least amount on their side of the room at the end of the game is the winner!

Cleaning up the paper is also fun. First, it's a game of basketball to get the paper in the box. Then, trying to cram as much paper as possible into one box requires all kinds of stomping inside the box. Children love this activity, too.

## Decorating

Don't wait to decorate. Decorating has a way of bringing order out of the chaos. This may sound like something that can wait, but I assure you it is important now. Children (and adults, too) have a need to be surrounded with something familiar. Moving is an upheaval on many different levels. Familiar knick-knacks and pictures provide a warm feeling of home and a sense of stability.

✓ Hang those pictures. Don't be afraid to hammer a nail into the wall. If you change your mind, a little spackle and paint will cover the hole. There's

79

nothing more depressing than a blank wall, or pictures just leaning against the wall waiting to be hung. This is your home; enjoy it and live in it now.

✓ Ask for help if you are not the "decorator type." My mother loves to visit my home and rearrange my furniture and objects d' art. She would probably come to your house, too.

✓ Girlfriends make great decorators. When one of our friends moved to a new house and was feeling overwhelmed, we had a "decorating party" for her. Everyone helped her unpack a few boxes and then created a decorating masterpiece. She was thrilled with the outcome.

✓ Magazines, or books on decorating, can provide some fun ideas. Look at pictures, decide what you like, and repeat it in your own home.

✓ There are all kinds of television shows these days that can inspire your "inner decorator." Take a break from unpacking, put your feet up, and watch for some fresh ideas. Or just fall asleep for a much-needed power nap.

## CHAPTER EIGHT

# First Things First

### Locate the Library

Finding the local public library is always our first "field trip" as a family. The library is filled with the most amazing resources, which you will desperately need right away. Also, the library is free, and after spending your life savings on moving, you will need something that doesn't cost you a cent.

✓ The internet is available for researching the area, or checking your e-mail if you don't have internet at home yet. When we moved to middle Tennessee, we had to wait three months for a telephone line. No, I am not exaggerating. The phone company was overwhelmed with new subdivisions being built, and we were low on their priority list. No matter how much I begged or pleaded, it still took them three months to hook up our telephone line, which also happened to provide our internet connection.

✓ DVD's and videos can be checked out for entertaining the children. Additionally, checking out books is fun for children, especially if they have not met any friends yet or it's summer and school is not in session.

✓ Research your destination. The library is full of travel books about places to go and fun things to do in the surrounding area. Pretend you are on a vacation and explore your new hometown.

✓ Check out books for you. A book on decorating or just a fun novel can be just what you need right now.

## Visit the Chamber of Commerce

Even the smallest of towns has its own Chamber of Commerce, or a Visitor Center. Their office will have free maps of the area, brochures about local attractions, and business directories. If you have not received your phone book yet, they might have that for you, too. It is their job to promote the town and local businesses, so they will have the answer to all kinds of questions. They are also generally quite hospitable and kind and by then you will be in want of a helpful friend.

The maps will be useful and your car might even be equipped with the fancy Global Positioning System (a.k.a. GPS); however, better than GPS are natives who have lived in the area their whole life. When we lived in Memphis, the school secretary was a long time Memphian. She was my own personal GPS. She was programmed into my phone for emergencies. I would call her from anywhere in the big city, then I would say in a very pitiful voice, "Help, I'm lost. I am at a stoplight next to a Walmart and across from Waffle House, but I can't see any street signs. Where am I?" She would always know exactly where I was, turn me around, and navigate the way back home for me. The kindness in her voice would also alleviate my state of fear and anxiety.

## Find the DMV

Your trip to the Department of Motor Vehicles (DMV) is more painful than a visit to the dentist. At least with a root canal you get painkillers. The lines at the DMV are always long, so plan to spend an entire day there; pack a picnic and bring a good book to read. Look online and carefully study the list of documents required and what kind of payment is accepted. We have visited the DMV twice in one week, because of forgotten items or not enough cash on hand.

When you arrive at the DMV, ask questions to be sure you are standing in the appropriate line. Speaking from experience, I assure you that there is nothing worse than waiting an hour in the wrong line.

At the end of the day you will have a new driver's license, car tags, and another license plate for your wall décor. At one time our garage wall was lined with license plates from NJ, KY, FL, TX, SC, TN, MO, and GA. And, yes, we really have lived in all of those states.

## Call the Doctor

This may not seem like something to do right away, but it's definitely better to be prepared. Our family always manages to need a doctor right away. On moving day, arriving at our new home in south Georgia, two of our boys came down with pneumonia. On other moves we have had asthma attacks and allergic reactions, and don't forget the infamous "threw-out-my-back" story. Again, be prepared.

## How To Move

- ✓ Call your previous doctor and ask for a referral to a new doctor. It's also a good idea to go ahead and request a copy of your medical records, especially those immunizations. Recently, I spent hours on the phone calling on past pediatricians from five different cities to find our five-year-olds' shot records. It turned out we had missed his four-year-old immunizations. Because of missing records, one of our sweet children (we won't name names) accidentally received the same immunizations twice. Thankfully it had no long-term effects (that we know of so far).
- ✓ Call your insurance company to see which doctors are on their list.
- ✓ Ask your new neighbors or co-workers whom they would recommend.
- ✓ Ask the librarian, or your new friend at the Chamber of Commerce, for some "gossip" about who the best doctors are in town. People love to talk, so listen well and you can gain great insights.
- ✓ Gather plenty of information before making a decision.

## Make a Friend

We all need friends, and we must put forth the effort in order for it to happen. You can sit at home feeling lonely or start looking for your new walking buddy. Maybe it's because I used to organize small groups for a living, but I enjoy seeing people gather together.

✓ Hosting a party right after you move is an especially radical and fun idea. People will be amazed at your hospitality. It's actually the easiest thing, because no one expects your house to be clean since you just moved. All the dishes and kitchen gadgets are still packed in boxes, so you are not expected to cook. One time we moved on Saturday of Memorial Day weekend and proceeded to have a huge pool party two days later. It was the easiest Memorial Day party I have ever hosted. I didn't have to do a thing to get ready for it. Everyone brought food for a cookout and we all had a relaxing and fun time.

✓ If throwing a party is too overwhelming for you, here are some other less intimidating ideas for initiating new friendships:

✓ Join the local athletic club and sign up for an exercise class.

## How To Move

✓ Start a neighborhood walking group or book club.

✓ Find some moms with children the same age and start a "play group." You can meet at a park, so no one feels the pressure to clean house.

✓ Take a plate of home-baked cookies or prepare a meal for the next new neighbor who moves into your subdivision.

✓ Sign up for a class in the community - sewing, cooking, gardening, etc.

✓ Invite a new acquaintance over for coffee and dessert. It takes less time and money to prepare. Also, in the evening light the "dust bunnies" are less visible, so don't worry as much about excessive cleaning.

✓ Volunteer for your favorite charity or non-profit group, and you will meet like-minded people with similar interests.

Get involved at your child's school. Your children will enjoy having you close by, since they are adjusting to their new environment. This is an excellent opportunity for you to become acquainted with the teacher, students, and other moms.

# CHAPTER NINE

# Culture Shock

According to Wikipedia, the definition of culture shock is "the anxiety and feelings of disorientation and confusion, felt when people have to operate within an entirely different cultural or social environment. It grows out of the difficulties of assimilating the new culture, causing difficulty in knowing what is APPROPRIATE." Take for instance the time we joined the Baptist church. When we stood before the congregation, the pastor asked my husband if he had anything to say. Being the talkative type, my husband proceeded to share a funny story about how he used to make fun of Baptists and how he certainly never dreamed he would become one. The southern congregation let out an uncomfortable laugh. Thankfully, they accepted us anyway, in spite of our many flaws.

## How To Move

With each of our twelve moves we have had much to learn about the culture we found ourselves living in. Although we never left the United States and the dominant language was always English, every move was like traveling to a foreign country.

## Language Barriers

Even if everyone speaks English, don't assume you won't experience language barriers. My husband grew up in New Jersey and we have spent the last fifteen years living in the south. I never know who is more shocked, us or the natives. When our daughter was in that "peek-a-boo" stage we were in a fancy restaurant. Some elegant southern ladies at the table behind us were admiring our daughter and enjoying a game of "peach pie" with her. When we got in the car, my husband, very confused, asked me, "Honey, why did those women keep saying 'peach pie' to Maddie?" Having grown up in southern culture, I was able to interpret the language for him and explain that they were actually saying "peep-eye", which is the southern version of peek-a-boo.

I recently learned that if you go shopping for

furniture, you will need to know the local pronunciations of common words. For example, if you are shopping for a new bedroom suite, this word may be pronounced "soot" or "sweet" depending on what part of the country you are living in.

Do not assume that anything is universally the same. You have probably seen, or been a part of, that line of cars after school, where mothers in mini vans are waiting for their children. Perhaps you have always heard it called the "carpool line." Well, in some places we have lived, it is known as the "pick up line," which I thought had something to do with single people at bars. The other unique name for it in some parts of America is the "hook up," which has that same odd connotation.

As you can see, culture shock is not a phenomenon reserved for people who travel overseas. I can testify to the high probability that every city in the United States is unique, culturally and socially. Every town has its own traditions and customs, and it's not always easy to figure out what those are and to find ways to fit in. We have experienced culture shock with every move, but we have also survived mostly unscathed by it.

Prepare yourself, because you too will experience the following stages of culture shock.

## Stage 1: Fun

This is the excitement and adventure stage of being in a new place. When we moved to Memphis we were lined up with the tourists at "Graceland" within the first week. Being a "tourist in your own town" is a great way to start your new adventure. Dads usually have a few days off before beginning their jobs, so it's the perfect time for a "vacation" in your new hometown. The Chamber of Commerce or Visitor Center will have all kinds of brochures about things to do and see. We have had the adventure of a lifetime visiting all kinds of museums, zoos, beaches, and parks.

Take out the map and draw a circle around the area where you live. You can take day trips to interesting places in the surrounding area. We can usually think of a fun day trip and travel up to four or five hours, which is the equivalent of two movies and one bathroom break.

Here's another great idea that my friends think is ingenious. When you take an excursion into unknown territory it is generally necessary to bring along food for everyone. You never know if you will find a Mc-Donalds in this uncharted land, so it's better to be prepared. For long car trips we make something called "Happy Sacks." This is the mom version of a "Happy Meal." Fill a brown paper lunch bag with your child's favorite foods and snacks, and be sure to include an inexpensive toy. I also like to decorate the outside of the sack. The meal is always more nutritious than greasy French fries, and you get to decide what kind of "toy" your child receives (like math flashcards, a new pencil, or stickers.) My children look forward to their "Happy Sacks" with excitement.

## Stage 2: Flight

Now is when reality sets in. You are not really on vacation. This is your home now and you have to accept that, but you have dreams about running away. On the inside you are screaming out that you just want to move back to what is familiar, but the thought of packing again squashes that idea pretty quickly. You look around and find yourself living among foreigners and aliens. Everyone and everything seems oddly different from anything that you have ever experienced before. You want to escape or turn back time, but your husband loves his new job and the kids are making new friends, so you just sit in the middle of the bedroom floor and cry your eyes out.

## Stage 3: Fight

This is not a pretty stage in the whole moving experience. This is when you become supremely critical and negative about everything and everyone. You can't stop talking about how things "used to be." You are not much fun to be around as you complain and gripe about every little thing you dislike. You have this terribly "Utopian" idea about how things were before you moved here. You might even fantasize about ways to sabotage your husband's success, so that your family can move back to the last place you last lived. (I know what you're wondering and that answer is no, I've never sabotaged my husband's job.)

You have only been here for 6 months, but the "locals" have lived here for three generations or more. You are trying to re-invent the town, but for some odd reason they are not receptive to all your great ideas. You may try desperately to re-create what you had before. You tell everyone, "Well, this is the way so-in-so does things," but for some strange reason no one is listening to you. It's time for a reality check; remember that YOU are the "alien" and not them.

## Stage 4: Fit

Now comes the moment of choice. You are at a crossroads; you can continue to isolate and alienate yourself, or find some creative ways to cope. Let's say you resign yourself to accept what fate has brought your way, which I have had to do twelve times. One definition of cultural fit is, "creative interaction with the new culture that includes a willingness to understand and embrace." No, you don't have to go around hugging people, but it's a good idea to work at making a friend or two. Think of creative ways to understand and adapt to this new "country" you find yourself in. What are the popular pastimes and entertainment in the area? Here are a few ideas to get you started:

- ✓ You have an extra long commute to school or work, so you buy some books on tape or check some out at the library, and enjoy the ride. We used to live exactly one mile from both work and school, but now we have a thirty minute commute. We can actually finish an entire game of car bingo. We also have more time to talk with our children about their day.
- ✓ You don't have pizza delivery, so you learn to make homemade dough. Homemade bread and grinding your own wheat was a popular pastime in Atlanta, so I succumbed and bought a wheat grinder. That's the most delicious bread I have ever eaten.
- ✓ You don't have any friends, so you join a book club.
- ✓ You don't have a bookstore with a coffee shop, so you search online for your favorite books while sipping on a cup of coffee and wearing your pj's.

✓ There are no therapists, so you write a book about moving and it's the best therapy you have ever experienced.

✓ You no longer live down the street from your momma, so you adopt a grandmother whose kids are living in Timbuktu. (By the way, my mom would like to be adopted. We have never lived near her and she misses us terribly. Remember, she'll also help you decorate.)

✓ You probably have gained a few pounds from all that "stress-eating," so you ask a neighbor to go walking with you a few times a week. You could also join an exercise class at the local gym and make some new friends.

# CHAPTER TEN

# Temporary Moves

## The "In-Between" Experience

We have had some interesting experiences with those unique "in-between" moves. You know the kind I am talking about: waiting for a house to be built or a house to sell, living with Mom and Dad to save money, short-term work assignments or the job that "wasn't-what-we-thought-it-would-be," or graduate school that leads to bigger and better opportunities in other places.

Now is not the time to hibernate; an adventure is waiting for you! You have to make the most of where you are. Consider this a unique opportunity to create fun experiences that you and your family will remember forever.

## Boxes Everywhere

When you know that this will be an "in-between" move, it's a wise idea to not unpack everything. The problem is you don't want to look at a bunch of cardboard boxes for months on end. If you can't afford a POD or a self-storage unit, then the boxes will be with you. Finding places to stack and store and hide them is essential to everyone's sanity. If there is no basement, garage, or attic, choose a large closet or a spare room to keep the boxes in one "out of the way" place.

If there is still no space to store the boxes, then cover them with some fun fabric, turn them into interesting décor, or hide them behind an attractive room divider. Try to make your temporary abode as comfortable as possible, in spite of the abundance of cardboard.

## Beware of Basement Storage

When my husband went back to graduate school in St. Louis, we found a very tiny rental house with a great basement, which we thought would make an excellent playroom for our four small children (ages 5, 3, 18 months, and 6 months, at the time). It turned out our children were petrified of the dark basement, but it was a superb storage area for all of our boxes. At least that was what we thought, until the basement flooded. Never having had a basement, we didn't know those things actually leak. The cracks in the walls are like tiny pipes that gush forth water during monsoon rains. Basements can still be good storage, but keep the boxes off the basement floor and away from the walls, especially those with suspicious-looking cracks.

## Bugs and boxes

One move, prior to the onslaught of children in our home, was to a small townhouse. This was temporary, since we were waiting for our new house to be built.

Now I have to tell you, in South Carolina they have a fancy name for roaches, Palmetto Bugs. They are just as ugly and, in fact, quite larger than they re in the north. If you tend to be a bit squeamish or faint of heart, you will want to skip the rest of this story and move on to the next section.

This particular townhouse, unbeknownst to us, had been infested with Palmetto Bugs because of the previous renters. We neatly stacked our boxes in a clever storage area under the steps. On moving day we did notice maybe one or two of these large tough bugs, but thought nothing of it. Day two and beginning to settle in, we noticed a few more Palmetto Bugs. We were not alarmed at that point, but did let the landlord know and she promised to send out the pest control company. We were pleased by her quick response to our "little" problem. Pest control came, they sprayed, and we were naïve.

At the end of the week the bugs seemed to have increased, rather than disappeared, and they were always alive instead of dead. We would see one crawl across the TV at night, such bold bugs they were. The scariest moment was turning on the kitchen light and watching them scurry to the dark corners of the room. Pest control returned for a much more serious spray. During that visit a lengthy conversation with the pest experts revealed the history of our town home and the interesting fact that roaches love to feed on the glue that holds cardboard boxes together.

Needless to say, we really love those large plastic storage tubs that we can purchase at discount stores. We are slowly, but surely, packing our belongings in those tubs, instead of cardboard held together with "roach food."

## Making the Most of It

Don't allow yourself to jump ahead in your mind to the next move, but enjoy the gift of today. We have made some of our dearest friends in places we stayed only a year, or less. We have seen every zoo and children's museum in every town we have ever lived, even before we had children. Create a fun and memorable experience for you and your family. Try these ideas for enjoying your current situation:

- ✓ Be a tourist and see all the local sights.
- ✓ Attend a class or learn a new hobby that is native to the area.
- ✓ Try every restaurant in town. You would not believe some of the unique places we have eaten across the country.
- ✓ Join a civic club or volunteer at a local charity.
- ✓ Get to know your neighbors; invite them over for coffee or start a book club.
- ✓ Check the newspaper for local events and then participate.
- ✓ Enjoy one another. When you are all alone in a new place this is the perfect opportunity to treasure the companionship of one another.

# CHAPTER ELEVEN

# The "Moving Blues"

**R**elocation makes the "top three" list of life's most stressful events. I have known many women who have never been sad in their lives, but surprisingly experienced some stage of depression after a move. If you maxed out your credit card in the first week, or you are consuming ice cream by the gallons, you may have a problem. When I inhale an entire package of oreos in one sitting (and no, I don't mean the snack size bag), then I know I am not doing well.

There are ranges of depression, from mild or temporary to very severe long-term depression. Don't ignore the signs and symptoms:

- ✓ Depressed or irritable mood most of the day
- ✓ Loss of interest or pleasure in activities

- ✓ A sudden change in weight, or a change in appetite
- ✓ Inability to sleep or sleeping too much, nearly every day
- ✓ Agitation or restlessness (observed by others) nearly every day
- ✓ Constant fatigue or loss of energy nearly every day
- ✓ Frequent feelings of worthlessness or inappropriate guilt
- ✓ Difficulty concentrating or making decisions nearly every day

## What Can You Do?

The first step is to talk to someone you trust about how you are feeling. They can help you decide if you need to get a professional opinion from a doctor or a counselor. You may have physiological symptoms that need to be treated. Stress does all sorts of crazy things to our bodies.

If you have a case of the "moving blues" that does not require assistance from a professional, then you may try some home remedies. Here are some fun and healthy ways to cope with the "moving blues" that do not involve eating or spending sprees:

- ✓ Go for a walk, because exercise and sunshine are both good "medicine."
- ✓ Rent a sad movie and cry your eyes out.
- ✓ Rent a funny movie about moving and laugh your head off.
- ✓ Attend a "Movers Anonymous" support group. (Ok, these don't really exist, but wouldn't it be great of they did?)
- ✓ Play a game with your kids, because for once in your life the phone won't be ringing since you don't have any friends yet.

✓ Write a book about moving, (hey, it worked for me). Or at least journal about your feelings and experiences.

✓ Join something. Force yourself to get out of the house and meet people. Even the smallest of towns has all sorts of book clubs, garden clubs, newcomers groups, athletic facilities, knitting circles, quilting bees, scrapbookers, and more. Activities are usually listed in the newspaper or at the Chamber of Commerce, or even at the local library. Just ask the librarian.

✓ Call an old friend who will encourage you, or your funny friend who makes you laugh, or the creative friend who will get you hooked on a hobby (If you move as much as we have, you will have friends in every time zone to call).

✓ Make a "gratitude list" of all the things in your life right now that make you happy. Try to think of one for every letter of the alphabet - A to Z. On one particular "downsize" move I was very sad about the "dream home" we had left behind. I made a list for myself of everything I was thankful for in our new home and taped it to my bathroom mirror, where I could see it and read it daily.

## How To Move

✓ Take a shower and get dressed - sounds so simple, but some days this is a HUGE accomplishment.

✓ Take a bubble bath and get lost in a good novel.

If the suggestions above do not cure the "blues" for you, then go back to step one and re-evaluate your emotional state:

*"Talk to someone you trust about how you are feeling. They can help you decide if you need to get a professional opinion from a doctor or a counselor."*

## CHAPTER TWELVE

# On the Road Again

You just received the news that you are moving again. What is it this time? Job transfer? Career change? Change of life? You did it before and you can do it again. In fact, now you're an experienced pro at this. Go back to the beginning of this book. Remember and laugh out loud at what happened on your last move.

- ✓ Embrace this new adventure.
- ✓ Learn from the mishaps of your previous move.
- ✓ Give away more stuff this time.
- ✓ Add a few more plastic storage bins and recycle some cardboard.
- ✓ Ask for help.
- ✓ Cry, laugh, and live.

## How To Move

You did it before and you CAN do it again. There is an adventure waiting for you right around the corner, and hopefully some new friends who will help you unpack when you get there. Who knows, this time you might have a neighbor who brings you that plate of warm chocolate chip cookies.

# APPENDIX A

# Where to Give It Away

### The Charity Guide
www.charityguide.org
*This is a comprehensive website that lists a variety of charities.*

### The Salvation Army
www.salvationarmyusa.org

### Goodwill Industries
www.goodwill.org
1-800-741-0186

### Vietnam Veterans of America
www.clothingdonations.org
*They will even pick up donations at your home.*

### Military Order of the Purple Heart Services Foundation

www.purpleheartpickup.org

*They also provide service to your door.*

### 1-800-Got Junk

*This service might cost a fee, but it's worth it.*

### Habitat for Humanity

www.habitat.org

1-800-HABITAT

*You can donate all kinds of building materials and appliances.*

# APPENDIX B

# Services to End

*Remember to include local club memberships and anything else you cannot use at your new location.*

| Service: | Phone No.: | Termination Date: |
|---|---|---|
| Water | | |
| Electricity | | |
| Gas | | |
| Telephone | | |
| Trash/Garbage | | |
| Recycling | | |
| Newspaper | | |
| Lawn Care | | |
| Auto Insurance | | |
| Home Insurance | | |
| | | |

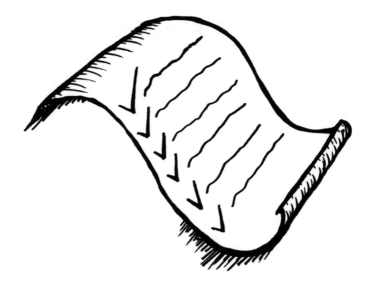

# APPENDIX C

# Services to Begin

| Service: | Phone No.: | Start Date: |
|---|---|---|
| Water | | |
| Electricity | | |
| Gas | | |
| Telephone | | |
| Trash/Garbage | | |
| Recycling | | |
| Newspaper | | |
| Lawn Care | | |
| Auto Insurance | | |
| Home Insurance | | |
| | | |
| | | |
| | | |

# APPENDIX D

# The Checklist for the Car

*Did you remember?*

✓ Emergency medicines: _____

_____

_____

_____

_____

_____

_____

✓ Pillows, favorite stuffed animals, and sleeping bags
✓ Change of clothes (or more)
✓ Nightlights and a lamp or two

- ✓ Coffee maker, filters, coffee, sugar, cream, and a mug
- ✓ Towels, shower curtain, and toilet paper
- ✓ Games or activities for the children
- ✓ Cleaning supplies
- ✓ Toolbox
- ✓ Important papers:_____

_____

_____

_____

_____

- ✓ A box of tissues
- ✓ Other "must haves"

_____

_____

_____

_____

_____

_____

_____

_____

## EPILOGUE

# Trainor Family Update

As this book heads to the publisher, we are about ten months into our current assignment in rural southeast Georgia. We don't have Starbucks or pizza delivery, but we are surviving on home brewed coffee and "hand tossed" pizzas (from the frozen food section of the grocery store).

Our family is quickly adjusting to this new country life. The children enjoy counting the horses, cows, and goats on the way to school each day. We can finish an entire game of auto bingo before arriving at school each morning. We have been pecan picking for the first time ever, and around here that is pronounced with a long e.

We are slowly learning the southeast Georgian language. We now know that "fixin' to" has absolutely nothing to do with tools or repairs. And if someone wants to "carry you" they are not talking about lifting you onto their shoulders for a ride on their back; they are simply offering to drive you somewhere in their car.

We have just purchased a few acres in the country, so we probably have another move in our future. We thank God for humor, love, and grace, as we embark on this wonderful adventure and another chapter in our lives.

## ABOUT THE AUTHOR:

Kathryn Trainor has a B.A. in Social Work and an M.A. in Education. She can de-clutter and pack a family of six, unpack within a week, and sew curtains for every room of the house by the end of the first month, all the while maintaining her sanity and southern charm.

Kathryn is the wife of Ted Trainor, a private school headmaster, who is an extremely experienced installer of mini blinds. They have four adorable and adventuresome children, who argue over where they were born. The Trainors have moved 12 times in 15 years, lived in five different states and ten cities, and have not lost their remote control.

# Index

# Order <u>more</u> copies of
# How To Move

If you've found this book helpful, you may want to order extra copies for your mobile family member, friends, and neighbors.

By Mail:
Make checks or money order payable to
Acclaim Press and mail to:

Acclaim Press
P.O. 238
Morley, Mo 63767
By Phone: (573) 472-9800
By Email: www.acclaimpress.com

Please send me:
_____ copies of *How To Move* at $12.95 each = $_____
_____ S&H $4 for 1st book & $1 ea./additional  $_____
_____ Sales tax $.78 ea. (GA residents only)    $_____
Total Enclosed = $ _____

Ship To:
Name_____
Address_____
City_____State_____ Zipcode_____
Phone_____ E-mail_____

Wholesale inquiries contact publisher.